Munchy

and

Jumpy Tales

VOLUME I

A Social Emotional Book for Kids about
Practicing Mindfulness, Finding Joy,
and Getting Second Chances

Read Aloud Stories for Children Age 5 - 8
and Their Grown Ups

Written by Noah Teitelbaum
Illustrated by Julia Gootzeit

Published by Empowering Education
383 Corona St.
Denver, CO 80218
(720) 766-5765
www.empoweringeducation.org

Written by Noah Teitelbaum

Illustrated by Julia Gootzeit

Book Design & Layout by Kory Kirby

ISBN 978-1-7349393-0-9

Printed in the United States of America

Contents

Note to Adults   v

A Forgotten Birthday Party   1

Paws and Hands   17

A Thorny Day   29

The Mixed-Up Friends   41

Note to Adults

In a couple of pages you'll meet Munchy and Jumpy as they learn to do "double-days," repeats of a day gone bad. (Have you seen the movie *Groundhog Day*?) These stories are part of Empowering Education's Social-Emotional Learning program. They are designed to be read aloud to children, enjoyed, and then discussed. Each story highlights a social emotional skill, including mindfulness, which is the act of paying attention to what's going on inside and around us.

At points in the stories, you'll find optional suggestions for movement or discussion. Look for these:

> *Let's sniff like*
> *Munchy does.*

> *How do you think*
> *Jumpy is feeling?*

Pick and choose which ones to use, based on how engaged your listeners are, their age, etc. Too many interruptions can prevent kids from becoming absorbed with the story, but questions or movement can also help squirmier readers stay engaged and go deeper with their thinking.

If you want some additional resources that go along with these stories or just to learn more about our program, which is available for K-8 schools, go to *empoweringeducation.org/book*

Let's go have some double-day adventures!

— Noah Teitelbaum, *Executive Director and Munchy and Jumpy fan*

1

A Forgotten Birthday Party

A long time ago, but not too long ago, and far away, but not too far away, lived twin rabbits, Munchy and Jumpy. They lived in a big tree in a park that was wild, but not too wild.

Today was the bunnies' birthday. The twins had many questions for their mother.

"*Momma,*" Jumpy asked, "*do you want to play my new game?*"

Munchy interrupted to ask, "*Do you think Toby Turtle will bring me chocolate carrots?*"

Mother didn't answer. She smiled and sent them outside to play.

Outside, Jumpy said to Munchy, *"I made these rings from leaves. The idea is to throw them onto someone's ears."* She tossed one into the air and onto her own ear. *"Ta-da! It's Rabbit-Ring Toss! We should play this with Toby!"*

She tossed a ring onto Munchy's ear. *"Ringo Bingo!"* she shouted.

Munchy smiled. *"You threw the ring and got my ear, but chocolate is what I hold most dear!"* He turned and saw Toby walking towards them with gifts.

"Happy Birthday!" Toby said and carried his gifts to the table. Munchy sniffed them.

Let's all sniff things just like Munchy!

"*Let's play Rabbit-Ring Toss!*" yelled Jumpy. She tossed a small loop into the air and watched it land on Munchy's ear. "*Ringo Bingo!*"

Jumpy explained the game to Toby. But when she said where to aim, Jumpy realized she couldn't see Toby's ears.

Toby said. "*Let's play hide-and-seek, instead. I'm good at that game!*"

"*But we always play hide-and-seek,*" Jumpy cried. "*I want to play this!*"

Mother told them to choose a game everyone could play. Jumpy crossed her arms, stuck out her bottom lip, and stood by herself.

How do you think Jumpy is feeling?

Munchy agreed to hide-and-seek. Instead of looking for Toby though, he went under the table and sniffed presents.

Soon, Mother brought out the cake. Jumpy joined them but stayed quiet. Munchy ate two pieces of cake and quickly opened presents. There were chocolate carrots for Munchy, just as he hoped. He stuffed a big one into his mouth. With a sore tummy, he left to lie down instead of saying goodbye to Toby.

After Toby left, Uncle Lamont came to wish the bunnies happy birthday. They told him about the party.

Uncle Lamont said. *"It sounds like you forgot to enjoy your party."*

"What does that mean?" Munchy asked.

"Munchy, you worried whether you'd get chocolate. And Jumpy, you were upset about not playing your game. You both forgot to enjoy yourselves."

"What should we do?" asked Jumpy. *"I don't want to forget to have fun."*

"Remember to enjoy your birthday party next year."

The bunnies felt tears in their eyes.

"Next year?" sniffed Jumpy. *"That's forever!"*

Uncle looked serious. *"There is a way, but it's pretty tricky. Get into bed and I'll tell you."*

Let's pretend to quickly get into our pajamas, brush our teeth, and crawl into bed.

Once in bed, their uncle told them the secret. *"Years ago, I learned a trick from a special hedgehog. If you have a day that doesn't go the way you want, you can say a special wish and live the day one more time."*

"What?!" said Jumpy, bouncing in bed. *"You get to do the day a second time?"*

Uncle said, *"Yes. But when you get a second chance, you must take three deep breaths and then pay close attention to what's happening around you and what you're feeling. Got it?"*

The bunnies nodded.

"Good. Now do exactly what I tell you."

Let's follow Uncle Lamont's instructions

"First, close your eyes and make tight fists with your paws. After you say the special words, take three deep breaths and open your eyes. Now repeat after me: Double-day, double day. Make it a double-day."

"Double-day, double-day, let us try another way."

The bunnies repeated the words and then took three deep breaths.

One. Two. Three.

Let's slowly breathe along with them and see how we feel

They opened their eyes. The bunnies were amazed to see Uncle Lamont was gone, and they were no longer in bed! Instead, they were at the start of their birthday party, and everything seemed more sparkly. They smelled the cake, felt the warm sun, and saw Toby walking towards their tree.

> *The bunnies are getting to do over part of their day!*
> *What do you think the bunnies will do differently at the*
> *party this time?*

Just like last time, Jumpy took her ring, tossed it into the air and caught it on her ear.

"Let's play Rabbit-Ring Toss!" she cried as Toby arrived.

And just like last time, she didn't see Toby's ears. But this time, Jumpy took a breath and noticed she was a bit upset she couldn't play her game. Then she looked at Toby and noticed he was embarrassed not to have big ears. Jumpy decided to play with Toby, and she joined the game of hide-and-seek.

Just like last time, Munchy went under the gift table when the game started. But this time, he looked up and stopped sniffing presents. He laughed at his sister's ears poking from her favorite hiding spot.

Later, as they ate birthday cake, the friends sang a silly song about a wolf who lost his pajamas and Jumpy laughed so hard that a bit of birthday cake came out of her nose. The bunnies had so much to tell their Uncle that night.

From that day on, the twin bunnies remembered the double-day trick. They used it often, but not too often. Maybe you can try it too.

The End

Discussion Questions:

1. Why did each of the bunnies not enjoy the birthday party?

2. What was different the second time they went through the day? What was the same?

3. What helped Munchy and Jumpy enjoy their birthday?

4. What is something that you did that should have been fun but you didn't actually enjoy, just like what happened to Munchy and Jumpy?

5. Munchy and Jumpy learned from their uncle about something we call mindfulness. Mindfulness means paying to what's going on inside of you and around you. We did it when we slowly breathed. How did that make you feel?

6. If you could do a double-day for one of the days that happened recently, what would you do differently?

For more resources for this story, go to
www.empoweringeducation.org/book

2

Paws and Hands

A long time ago, but not too long ago, and far away, but not too far away, lived twin rabbits, Munchy and Jumpy. They lived with their mother in a cozy tree that was tall, but not too tall, in a park that was wild, but not too wild.

While exploring the park one day, Munchy and Jumpy saw a big tree with low branches that swayed in the wind. Animals swung from the branches and sounds of laughter grew as the bunnies hopped closer.

Jumpy's eyes lit up when she saw a small kangaroo and a squirrel with small wings speeding through the branches. She jumped into the branches to join their game.

> *Jump in place with your arms out like the flying squirrel or pull your arms in tight and jump like a kangaroo.*

Munchy watched his sister play and then looked at his paws, which didn't seem well-suited for climbing vines. His sister and her new friends waved for him to join their game—they called it Jump Chase— but he turned away, suddenly interested in a bug on the ground. His cheeks turned warm, and his stomach felt strange and shaky. He hoped everyone would stop looking at him.

Why did Munchy start looking at a
bug when the animals looked at him?

He then saw a raccoon reaching for a branch. She skipped around
and tried others, but all were too high.

Let's pretend to reach for a branch.

The raccoon sat down and noticed Munchy. *"Hi, I'm Rhonda,"* she said. *"That game makes me nervous, too."*

Munchy saw fur around her eyes like a mask. He looked away and said, *"Uhh, hi."* His stomach felt shaky and his cheeks still warm. *"I saw a tasty sweet onion over there. See you later,"* Munchy said, walking to the other side of the tree. Rhonda watched him, and her shoulders dropped as she looked down.

How do you think Rhonda felt?

As Munchy ate an onion, he wondered what it would be like to swing on the branches. It could be fun to play with Rhonda, but she looked like a robber with that mask on her face. *"I really like playing with other rabbits best,"* he decided.

Why do you think Munchy decided he wants to play only with other rabbits?

Later that day, as the bunnies walked home, Jumpy talked about the best way to catch a flying squirrel. *"If you pretend to eat a nut, they come over every time!"* she said, laughing. *"Who did you meet?"* she asked.

Munchy told his sister he spent most of the day eating onions. He mentioned meeting a raccoon but didn't think he should play with animals other than rabbits, especially those with masks on their faces.

"We have lots of different-looking friends," said Jumpy *"Toby the turtle doesn't have ears that I can see. But he's one of my best friends!"* Jumpy took Munchy's paw. *"It's great to play by yourself,"* she said. *"But it seems like you didn't want to play alone."*

That night, Jumpy was exhausted from playing Jump Chase and fell asleep the moment they got into bed. Munchy lay awake thinking about the day. He should have said more to Rhonda. He wanted a double-day, to try the day over again. He closed his eyes, squeezed his paws, and said the special words.

Let's repeat after Munchy.

"Double-day, double-day, make it a double-day.
Double-day, double-day, let me try another way."

Munchy remembered what his uncle told him, sat up straight, and took three deep breaths.

Let's breathe with him.

One. Two. Three.

When he unclenched his fists and opened his eyes, he was back under the big tree. His sister played Jump Chase. Everything was a little more sparkly.

What do you think Munchy will
do differently this time?

Just like last time, Munchy looked away when Jumpy called for him to play. Just like last time, he spotted Rhonda. And just like last time, she said, *"Hi, I'm Rhonda. That game makes me nervous, too."*

But this time, Munchy noticed two feelings. He felt nervous about being friends with a raccoon, but he also felt curious. *"Hi, I'm Munchy."*

Rhonda held up her paws. *"I've got good hands for gripping and swinging, but I can't jump very high."*

Munchy smiled and said, *"I can jump, and you can grip, but if we try to swing, we'll both just slip!"* Rhonda laughed but then stopped. Munchy's rhyme gave her an idea!

Rhonda climbed the tree to find a thick branch. Munchy jumped and pushed the swinging branches toward her. She grabbed them with her hands. One-by-one she tied the branches.

Let's tie some branches together.

Rhonda double-checked her knots, climbed into the tangle of branches, and let them swing into the air. Munchy looked up and saw what they had made. A hammock!

As Munchy jumped to join Rhonda, other animals came to investigate. With Munchy and Rhonda's permission, everyone took turns in the hammock to swing fast, but not too fast. Munchy and Jumpy and their new friends laughed and swung high, but not too high, until late into the afternoon.

The End

Discussion Questions:

1. Why didn't Munchy want to play with Rhonda?

2. What did Rhonda and Munchy have in common? What were the differences?

3. What did Munchy do differently during the double-day?

4. How were the differences between Rhonda and Munchy helpful?

5. How are some of your friends different from you?

6. When has it been hard for you to talk with new people? How do you handle that?

For more resources for this story, go to
www.empoweringeducation.org/book

3

A Thorny Day

A long time ago, but not too long ago, and far away, but not too far away, there lived twin rabbits, Munchy and Jumpy. They lived in a cozy hole in a tree that kept them warm while they slept, but not too warm.

The rabbits awoke to the sound of raindrops. Tip, tap, tip, tap. They snuggled under their blanket. Jumpy suddenly sat up and cried, *"Today I run in the Great Field Race!"*

"Sorry," Mother said. *"The race is cancelled because of rain."*

Jumpy's heart sank. She threw herself onto the bed. *"I can run in the rain! I'm faster than raindrops!"* She jumped from bed and sped outside.

Outdoors, she stomped her foot.

"*Jumpy, that wasn't nice,*" scolded Mother.

"*Frogs like water,*" Jumpy pouted.

Once Jumpy was inside and dry, she and Munchy sat at the window. The steady raindrops now sounded tippety-tap, tippety-tap, tippety-tap.

Munchy chewed a tasty radish. Jumpy tapped one foot.

By lunchtime, Jumpy tapped both feet, both paws, and—somehow—one of her ears. *"Ugh! This is the worst day ever."*

Just then, lightning filled the sky!

SHACRAM!

"Thunder!" said Jumpy, leaping. *"Oh, thunder is the best!"*

Munchy hid and shook under the blanket. He quickly ate a handful of strawberries.

Then again: Flash, SHACRAM! Munchy added a pillow over his head.

Another crash. Then another! Munchy's teeth chattered as he stuffed three more strawberries into his mouth.

Can you make your teeth chatter and pretend to eat?

Finally, the thunder and lightning stopped, but the rain continued. Jumpy tapped impatiently and Munchy hid under his pillow. He was out of strawberries, so he chewed on his stuffed giraffe. Soon, Munchy held his belly and groaned.

> *What do you think each of the bunnies is feeling?*

Later, as Mother tucked them into bed, she asked if they wanted to do roses and thorns.

"What's that?" Munchy asked.

"We say the best thing that happened—the rose—and the hardest thing—the thorn," Mother explained.

"It was all thorns," said Jumpy. *"I hated today. I missed my race, and we just sat around."*

"Yeah, the day was one big thorn!" agreed Munchy. *"That thunder was loud and scary. And I ate too much."*

> *Can you think of any roses during Munchy's and Jumpy's days—anything that they enjoyed—that they are forgetting?*

Mother said, *"When I'm having a hard day, I like to sing."*

"You have thorny days, too?" asked Munchy. *"But you're our momma!"*

Mother laughed. *"Yes, I do. If the day is really hard, I imagine standing on a big head of lettuce, gently swaying in the breeze."*

"Maybe you two should decide what makes you feel better."

The bunnies thought about that as Mother kissed them goodnight.

What are some things that make you feel better when you're having a thorny or tough day?

As they lay in bed thinking, Jumpy whispered to Munchy, *"Let's do that day over."*

"Let's!" said Munchy. They closed their eyes, squeezed their paws tightly and said the words they had learned.

> Let's do this with the bunnies.

"Double-day, double-day, make it a double-day. Double-day, double-day, let us try another way."

They sat up straight and took three deep breaths.

> Let's breathe with them.

One, two, three. They opened their eyes, and everything felt more sparkly. Just like last time, the bunnies watched the rain fall and puddle on the ground. Just like last time, they saw the dark gray clouds in the sky. And just like last time, they heard the fast tippety-tap, tippety-tap, tippety-tap.

What do you think the bunnies will do differently this time when they have a rainy day?

"I want to do something!" Jumpy exclaimed, tapping her foot. But this time, she grabbed a small ball from her toy box and squeezed.

Let's turn one of our hands into a ball and squeeze it with the other.

Jumpy's foot relaxed. She spied her coloring book and opened it to color.

Just then, lightning lit the room again and SHACRAM! Thunder shook the tree. Munchy jumped under the blankets. But this time, he called, *"Mom, that thunder is too loud."*

Mother picked him up and squeezed.

Let's each squeeze ourselves tightly, in a big hug.

He smiled and said, *"I want a lot of strawberries."* But then he changed his mind. *"No, I need just one strawberry. And I would love you to sing two songs. And give me three hugs."*

And that's what Mother did. She gave him one juicy strawberry, sang two songs, and hugged him three times. The bunnies felt snug and calm with Mother in their tree that was small, but not too small, and warm, but not too warm, as they listened to the rain fall.

The End

Discussion Questions

1. What was each of the bunnies feeling during the rainy day? How do you know?

2. What did each bunny do to feel better?

3. The things that you do when you are having a tough day are called "coping skills." What is a coping skill that makes you feel better? When is a good time to use it?

4

The Mixed-Up Friends

A long time ago, but not too long ago, and far away, but not too far away, lived twin rabbits, Munchy and Jumpy. They lived with their mother in a cozy tree that was big, but not too big, in a park that was wild, but not too wild.

One day, Munchy and Jumpy waited with Uncle Lamont for their friends to arrive in the park. Uncle had set up a scavenger hunt with clues.

Their friends soon arrived. Lizzie the Lizard ran fast, ready for action. Wally the Wizard, a thoughtful brown mouse, calmly walked toward the tree wearing his special hat.

Uncle Lamont told the friends they should split into two groups. Each group would look for a hidden object.

Jumpy admired how fast Lizzie ran and paired with her. Munchy teamed with Wally, who was very smart. Each group received a clue.

Munchy read their clue:

> *You through the door I will let,*
> *and you can bet that I've been set,*
> *right where cow tongues get wet.*

Munchy and Wally thought about their clue.

Let's scratch our heads and think about the clue.

"Do you have cows?" asked Wally.

"Rabbits don't have cows! But the farmer across the field does! He has an old bathtub he fills with water where their tongues get wet! What does it mean, 'you through the door I will let'?"

"I know," said Wally. *"A key!"*

"Yes!" shouted Munchy. They raced to find the bathtub.

The empty tub nestled in the grass, next to a water barrel.

How could they climb into the tub? Wally had an idea. He would cling to Munchy's back, while Munchy jumped.

But when Munchy jumped, his foot knocked the barrel. Fortunately, the friends bounced into the tub. Unfortunately, the water barrel tipped, and water started pouring into the tub!

"Should we jump out or try to swim?" asked Wally.

"I don't know!" said Munchy. *"We don't have time to think!"* The rabbit and mouse scrambled to the far end. Water poured, and soon they were swimming.

Let's use our arms to swim and stay afloat in the bathtub!

Luckily, Munchy's foot pulled up the bathtub stopper. The water drained, and Wally and Munchy lay wet and exhausted at the bottom. Once they caught their breath, the friends grabbed the key and made their way to Uncle Lamont.

Back at the tree, Jumpy and Lizzie had their own clue:

If you roam near the foam,
you will find this once shiny stone.

"That's easy!" Jumpy shouted. *"Uncle Lamont hid my pet rock near the foamy stream!"*

At the stream, they saw Toby the Turtle.

"Hey!" said Jumpy. *"I think that's my rock! Is he...?"*

Before Jumpy could finish, Lizzie yelled, *"Let's get that rock-steal-ing turtle!"* She bounded down the hill, jumped onto his shell with her sticky hands, and smacked Toby with her tail. In surprise, Toby started to shake.

> Let's curl up like turtles and try to shake
> Lizzie off our backs.

Fortunately, turtle shells are quite hard. Unfortunately, Lizzie's tail swung and hit Toby's eye.

"Ow! What are you doing?" cried Toby.

"She's stopping a stone-stealing!" yelled Jumpy.

"Stealing?" said Toby. *"I'm not stealing. I was returning your pet rock."*

"Exactly!" cried Lizzie, who wasn't really listening. *"You're a thief."*

Lizzie eventually understood Toby was not stealing the rock, and she climbed off his back to apologize. Toby tried to smile, but there were tears in both his eyes. He didn't accept Jumpy's invitation for cookies and tea.

Back at the tree, the teammates handed the key and stone to Uncle Lamont. Wally wrung water from his hat and left, looking sad. Lizzie hung her head and murmured, *"I hope Toby's okay,"* before she left. The twins ate dinner and headed to bed.

"I really like Lizzie," Jumpy said. *"She's so fast! But she never stops to think, and now Toby's hurt and sad."*

"We almost drowned today," said Munchy, *"because Wally and I couldn't act fast enough in the bathtub. I could have used Lizzie."*

"And I could have used Wally," said Jumpy. *"He wouldn't have attacked Toby."*

The bunnies knew it was time for a double-day! They closed their eyes and clenched their paws.

> Close your eyes, squeeze your
> hands and repeat after me.

"Double-day, double-day, make it a double-day.
Double-day, double-day, let us try another way."

They took three deep breaths.

> Let's breathe with them.

One. Two. Three.

When they opened their eyes, everything was sparkly. They were back with Uncle Lamont, choosing teams. Jumpy chose Wally because he was thoughtful. Munchy paired with Lizzie, who acted quickly.

Just like last time, Munchy got the clue leading to the bathtub. Just like last time, they jumped into the tub. And just like last time, Munchy knocked over the barrel and water poured. But this time, he was with Lizzie. When she saw the water, she grabbed Munchy's paw and shouted, *"Jump!"* From the top, they watched the tub fill and didn't get wet. Munchy spotted the key and Lizzie dove, grabbed it with her tongue, and climbed out with her sticky lizard hands.

Let's pretend to climb out of the
tub with our sticky hands.

Just like last time, Jumpy got the clue leading to her pet rock at the
stream. Just like last time, she saw Toby the turtle with the rock.
And just like last time, Jumpy said, *"Hey! I think that's my rock!"*

But this time, nobody interrupted. *"Is he taking my rock? Why would Toby do that?"*

Wally asked Toby, who explained, *"I was just taking this rock back to Jumpy! Here you go!"* Feeling lucky to have such a good friend, Jumpy invited the turtle back to their house.

Everyone met at the house for radish tea and cookies. The cookies were crunchy, but not too crunchy, and sweet, but not too sweet, and even Toby had seconds.

The End

Discussion Questions:

1. What was Lizzie the Lizard good at? Which part of our brain is like that? (The lizard brain or amygdala.)

2. What was Wally the Wizard good at? Which part of our brain is like that? (The wizard brain or prefrontal cortex.)

3. Why was it a problem for Jumpy to have Lizzie as her partner?

4. Why was it a problem for Munchy to have Wally as his partner?

5. When would you want Lizzie the Lizard to help you?

6. When would you want Wally the Wizard to help you?

For more resources for this story, go to
www.empoweringeducation.org/book

About the Authors

Noah Teitelbaum was a school teacher and teacher-trainer, and is now the Executive Director of Empowering Education. He lives in Denver with his wife and two children, Lilly Mae and Jonah, who helped develop these stories.

Julia Gootzeit is a cartoonist and illustrator living in North Carolina. She loves hanging out with her cats, and trying new recipes. You can find more of her work at juliagootzeit.com

CPSIA information can be obtained
at www.ICGtesting.com
Printed in the USA
LVHW072112160123
737254LV00009B/298

9 781734 939309